I like to sum up inductive study this way. We've drawn a big poster for our students that shows a man going fishing. The caption reads, "Give me a fish and I'll eat for a day. Teach me to fish, and I'll feed for a lifetime." Inductive Bible study is simply a way of teaching people how to fish. It's teaching ordinary folk some simple methods of observing and thinking through what they read, so that they know how to study the Word of God for themselves.

Norman Bell

"I had perceaved by experyence, how that it was impossible to stablysh the laye people in any truth, excepte the scripture were playnly layde before their eyes in their mother tonge, that they might se the processe, ordre and meaninge of the texte. . . . "

William Tyndale (1494? -1536)

TEACHING THE BIBLE FROM THE INSIDE OUT

David C. Cook Publishing Co.

ELGIN, ILLINOIS—WESTON, ONTARIO

Published by David C. Cook Publishing Co., Elgin, IL 60120
Edited by Linda Girard and Sharrel Keyes
Designed by Kurt Dietsch

Printed in the United States of America
Library of Congress Catalog Number: 78-61300
ISBN: 0-89191-160-X

CONTENTS

IN THE LABORATORY WITH AGASSIZ:

The Inductive Idea

Let's start with a story—a story about a famous teacher, a famous student, and a famous fish.

The professor is Louis Agassiz, one of the great natural scientists of the nineteenth century. The setting is Yale University; the year is about 1858. The student, Samuel Scudder, later became a well-known entomologist himself. And the fish? Well, that's where this story begins. . . .

As you read "In the Laboratory with Agassiz," ask yourself what this student's experience has to teach the person who is serious about Bible study.

In the Laboratory with Agassiz
SAMUEL H. SCUDDER

It was more than 15 years ago that I entered the laboratory of Professor Agassiz and told him I had enrolled my name in the scientific school as a student of natural history.

"When do you wish to begin?" he asked. "Now," I replied.

"Very well," he reached from a shelf a huge jar of specimens in yellow alcohol.

"Take this fish," said he, "and look at it: we call it a Haemulon; by and by I will ask you what you have seen."

In ten minutes I had seen all that could be seen in that fish, and started in search of the professor, who had, however, left the museum; and when I returned, after lingering over some of the odd animals stored in the upper apartment, my specimen was dry all over. I dashed the fluid over the fish as if to resuscitate it from a fainting fit, and looked with anxiety for a return of a normal, sloppy appearance. This little excitement over, nothing was to be done but return to a steadfast gaze at my mute companion. Half an hour passed, an hour, another hour; the fish began to look loathsome. I turned it over and around; looked it in the face–ghastly; from behind, beneath, above, sideways, at a three-quarter view–just as ghastly. I was in despair; at an early hour I concluded that lunch was necessary; so with infinite relief, the fish was carefully replaced in the jar, and for an hour I was free.

On my return, I learned that Professor Agassiz had been at the museum, but had gone and would not return for several hours. My fellow students were too busy to be disturbed by continued conversations. Slowly I drew forth that hideous fish, and with a feeling of desperation again looked at it. I might not use a magnifying glass; instruments of all kinds were interdicted. My two hands, my two eyes, and the fish; it

8

seemed a most limited field. I pushed my fingers down its throat to see how sharp its teeth were. I began to count the scales in the different rows until I was convinced that that was nonsense. At last a happy thought struck me—I would draw the fish; and now with surprise I began to discover new features in the creature. Just then the professor returned.

"That is right," he said. "A pencil is one of the best eyes."

With these encouraging words he added, "Well, what is it like?"

He listened attentively to my brief rehearsal of the structure of parts whose names were still unknown to me: the fringed gill-arches and movable operculum; the pores of the head, fleshy lips, and lidless eyes; the lateral line, the spinous fins, and forked tail; the compressed and arched body. When I had finished, he waited as if expecting more, and then, with an air of disappointment.

"You have not looked very carefully; why," he continued, more earnestly, "you haven't seen one of the most conspicuous features of the animal, which is as plainly before your eyes as the fish itself; look again, look again!" And he left me to my misery.

I was piqued; I was mortified. Still more of that wretched fish! But now I set myself to my task with a will, and discovered one new thing after another, until I saw how just the professor's criticism had been. The afternoon passed quickly and when, toward its close, the professor inquired, "Do you see it yet?"

"No," I replied, "I am certain I do not, but I see how little I saw before."

"That is next best," said he, earnestly.

The cordial greeting from the professor the next morning was reassuring; here was a man who seemed to be quite as anxious as I, that I should see for myself what he saw.

"Do you perhaps mean," I asked, "that the fish has symmetrical sides with paired organs?"

Samuel H. Scudder, *Every Saturday* (April 4, 1874).

He was thoroughly pleased, "Of course, of course!"
I ventured to ask what I should do next.
"O, look at your fish!" he said, and left me again to my own devices. In a little more than an hour he returned and heard my new catalogue.
"That is good, that is good!" he repeated, "but that is not all; go on"; and so, for three long days, he placed that fish before my eyes, forbidding me to look at anything else, or to use any artificial aid. "Look, look, look," was his repeated injunction.
This was the best entomological lesson I ever had–a lesson whose influence has extended to the details of every subsequent study; a legacy the professor has left to me, as he left it to many others, of inestimable value, which we could not buy, with which we cannot part.

What was that "lesson of inestimable value" that Agassiz' student learned?

He learned how to use careful, orderly observation on that fish in order to draw out much more than he had ever thought possible. The result was a lesson about *how to learn* that stayed with him all his life.

Look back at the things the student did to observe that "ghastly" fish. He stared at it, poked it, fingered it, sloshed alcohol over it, stuck his finger down its throat, counted its scales, and even tried to draw the fish. The longer he looked at it, the more intelligent and resourceful he became in seeing how to observe.

FACTS TO CONCLUSIONS

To approach a subject inductively—whether it's a fish, or a love letter—simply means that we gather all the facts (observation), see how they relate (understanding), and then draw conclusions from those facts (generalization). After those steps, we do something because of what we've learned (application).

For example, I see that the sky has clouded over. I hear thunder in the distance. I feel a few drops on my head. I pull these facts together and conclude that it's going to rain. Then, on the basis of my conclusion, I make a response. In this case, I put up my umbrella, or run for shelter. That's the inductive process.

Definition: Inductive Bible study is an approach to Bible study that helps us observe the Scripture directly, in context. Beginning with the Bible itself, we learn how to dig into a passage on our own and see much more than we did at first view. Then we relate and interpret the facts and make appropriate application. Once mastered, inductive Bible reading becomes the checkpoint for every other kind of Bible reading or study we might do.

It's helpful to think of the inductive approach to the Bible as an attitude. Catherine Schell, one of the contributing teachers for this book, tells us this story:

> I once read an interesting mystery story called **The Gossip Truth** by Jonathan Burke. In the story, a young reporter comes to a detective who is working on a murder case. The reporter, eager to get her story, says, "It's very difficult for me to know what's relevant in this case unless I know what line of investigation you're pursuing. In my line of business," she continues, "we like to establish the general approach before we fit in the details."
>
> The detective replies, "You mean your editor lays down his prejudices and the rest of you make the facts fit the policy?"

"Certainly not!" the reporter says. "But to get a coherent pattern out of anything. . . ."

"The details make the pattern," the detective interrupts, "not the other way around. It's a matter of drudgery and maybe, once in a while, a stroke of luck. You just collect as many bits and pieces as you can and discover how they naturally fit together and what meaning you can draw from the relationship to each other."

I think this sums up the inductive approach.

Catherine Schell
Contributing Teacher

Look back at that reporter a moment. What she wanted was a pattern or an idea that would tell her ahead of time what to look for in the case. She wanted to know right now, beforehand, which clues were important, and which ones to ignore.

That wish is natural. We are comfortable when we can use our accepted, familiar ideas to interpret any new fact we discover. But, says the detective, it can be dangerous. It may mean we fail to solve the case correctly.

Inductive study helps us come to the Bible like the detective rather than the reporter. God didn't give us the conclusions; He gave us the materials to reach them with. God chose to give us the Bible as *data:* a series of stories, history, poetry, prophecy, and letters, rather than as a theological treatise or set of conclusions organized in outline form.

So God has made it possible for every believer to begin to "own the data" as soon as he can read, to begin to move from the inside out. By studying the Bible inductively, we let God give us the facts in context. We show to God and to ourselves that we are more interested in what He says than in what we or others think He ought to say.

12

CHARACTERISTICS OF INDUCTIVE STUDY

- Inductive Bible study is a study of a unit of Scripture, usually a book, or a portion that is relatively complete in itself. We do not focus on a book *about* the Bible, or a book about a topic or problem, which uses the Bible for reference or to support points being made.

- Inductive study deliberately begins digging into that one passage or book, without leaning on commentaries, outside opinions from Bible experts, last week's sermon, or even other parts of the Bible. God wants us to continue reading His Word throughout our lives so that He can give us new, larger understandings and fresh revelation, and sometimes, to correct a hazy or wrong idea we may hold.

- Inductive Bible study has a different goal than devotional reading, and should not replace or be confused with devotional reading. In devotional reading, we approach a short passage looking for one good idea or one uplifting thought for the day. But when we study inductively, we come to the Scripture in a different way. We spend more time with observation, and we judge everything in context. In a fresh way, we see how it fits in its place, understand what it means, and then decide what God wants us to do.

- Inductive study moves carefully through the three stages: observation, understanding, generalization. We do not try to do these all at once, but go through a *process*. And that process is one we must understand if we are to be good teachers.

- Every inductive study is concerned first to see the whole, big picture, and then to see how this divides naturally into parts.

FORMS OF INDUCTIVE STUDY

Inductive study takes different forms. Let's look at three variations, ranging from total independence to a fully guided approach:

- The **pure form,** sometimes called the *manuscript method,* is most like the Agassiz story. A book of the Bible, typed out without paragraph or verse divisions, is the "fish." The reader takes this manuscript, some blank notepaper, and a pencil. With only these tools, and an attentive mind and eye, you discover the main thought divisions, divide the passage into paragraphs and major units, summarize the main points, and continue the process by observing, relating and generalizing, moving one natural paragraph or section at a time.

- A **partially guided** form of inductive study does not abandon you with just a "fish" and some paper, but would not make up all the questions for you, either. Beginning questions help you observe the whole, divide it, give titles, then tackle each section. Then, you would answer some further questions and find clues to raise others yourself, part by part. This moderately guided, somewhat open-ended approach is the one we follow for our sample study on the Book of Jonah.

- A **fully guided** form of inductive study will supply a series of specific questions for groups or persons to use in investigating a Bible passage or book. The nature of the discussion questions leads the group into the text to discover, observe, relate ideas, and generalize. Several good series of inductive Bible study guides are available in most Christian bookstores. Three of our contributing teachers have written such guides. You'll find titles listed in the appendix.

DIGGING IN

*A Sample Study for Teachers
on the Book of Jonah*

The best way to learn to swim, to ride a bicycle, or to fish is to learn while you *do* it. So—let's see how the inductive process works on a Bible passage. In this sample study, we'll concentrate on three goals: 1) to learn what we mean by *observation* in a Bible study, 2) to learn what kinds of questions are inductive, and 3) to see how *context* (or reading a passage in its place) is important in understanding any part of the Bible.

We've used words like "observation," "fact," and "clue" to suggest where inductive study starts.

In approaching a passage of Scripture by the inductive process, we will do just what the student did with his fish, or the detective with his clues, only we do it to words rather than to scales, or fingerprints. We will look at it carefully for significant facts.

Budding newspaper writers learn the "five W's" as a basis for thorough investigating and reporting: Who? What? Where? When? Why?

Here is a general list of questions, using those "five W's," and a sixth question, "How," that you would use to begin tackling any part of Scripture inductively.

- **What** kind of writing is this? (Letter, poem, historical account, narrative, prophecy.)
- **What** parts can we see?
- **Who** are the people involved? (In a letter, or thought passage this means, who is writing to whom? Who is mentioned in the letter? In a prophecy, who is the specific historical audience spoken to? What does the speaker say about himself? about God? about his audience? In a story, who are the characters, and who is telling the story to whom?) For every pronoun, who is meant? For example, when John says in I John 1:1, "we have seen it," who is *we*?
- **What** is happening?
- **When** is all this happening? (This does not mean a date or year unless indicated in the text. It means at what point in the ministry of Jesus? Or, after what and before what other events in the Bible? Or, at what time of day—whatever the text itself says about time.)
- **Where** is the action taking place? (What country, or at whose house, and what does the setting tell you?)
- **Why?** Does one event or person cause something else to happen? What are the motives and feelings here?
- **How** does each of the parts relate to the whole portion of Scripture?
- **How** is the story or argument being told or arranged?
- **What** are the author's tactics? **Why** did he write this? Is he persuading, reporting, worshiping, teaching?
- **What** was the writer's train of thought in this passage?

You'll find all these basic questions turning up in more specific ways, as you move through the sample study.
Think of each kind of question as a magnet that can help you pick up all the clues.

Now, let's begin!

On the next three pages, you'll find the Book of Jonah reprinted from the New English Bible without the verse or chapter marks. Here's what to do:

1. Find a quiet corner, a pencil, and plenty of paper, and give yourself about a half hour. Of course, you may decide you like the exercise so much that you take longer. But in 30 minutes of uninterrupted time, you can get the basics.

2. Ask God for an open heart.

3. Read the whole book through completely, to get the whole picture in mind.

4. Now you're ready to write. Put in one sentence the whole thrust or main point of the book.

5. Now read the book again, and begin writing down your answers to the inductive questions. Use the suggested questions to help you form your *own* good questions.

The Book of Jonah

THE WORD OF THE LORD CAME TO JONAH son of Amittai: 'Go to the great city of Nineveh, go now and denounce it, for its wickedness stares me in the face.' But Jonah set out for Tarshish to escape from the Lord. He went down to Joppa, where he found a ship bound for Tarshish. He paid his fare and went on board, meaning to travel by it to Tarshish out of reach of the Lord. But the Lord let loose a hurricane, and the sea ran so high in the storm that the ship threatened to break up. The sailors were afraid, and each cried out to his god for help. Then they threw things overboard to lighten the ship. Jonah had gone down into a corner of the ship and was lying sound asleep when the captain came upon him. 'What, sound asleep?' he said. 'Get up, and call on your god; perhaps he will spare us a thought and we shall not perish.'

At last the sailors said to each other, 'Come and let us cast lots to find out who is to blame for this bad luck.' So they cast lots, and the lot fell on Jonah. 'Now then,' they said to him, 'what is your business? Where do you come from? What is your country? Of what nation are you?' 'I am a Hebrew,' he answered, 'and I worship the Lord the God of heaven, who made both sea and land.' At this the sailors were even more afraid. 'What can you have done wrong?' they asked. They already knew that he was trying to escape from the Lord, for he had told them so. 'What shall we do with you,' they asked, 'to make the sea go down?' For the storm grew worse and worse. 'Take me and throw me overboard,' he said, 'and the sea will go down. I know it is my fault that this great storm has struck you.' The crew rowed hard to get back to land but in vain, for the sea ran higher and higher. At last they called on the Lord and said, 'O Lord, do not let us perish at the price of this man's life; do not charge us with the death of an innocent man. All this, O Lord, is thy set purpose.' Then they took Jonah and threw him overboard, and the sea stopped raging. So the crew were filled with the fear of the Lord and offered sacrifice and made vows to him. But the Lord ordained that a great fish should swallow Jonah, and for three days and three nights he remained in its belly.

Jonah prayed to the Lord his God from the belly of the fish:
I called to the Lord in my distress,
    and he answered me;
out of the belly of Sheol I cried for help,
    and thou hast heard my cry.
Thou didst cast me into the depths, far out at sea,
    and the flood closed round me;
all thy waves, all thy billows, passed over me.
I thought I was banished from thy sight
and should never see thy holy temple again.
    The water about me rose up to my neck;
        the ocean was closing over me.
    Weeds twined about my head
        in the troughs of the mountains;
        I was sinking into a world
    whose bars would hold me fast for ever.

But thou didst bring me up alive from the pit, O Lord my God.
As my senses failed me I remembered the Lord,
and my prayer reached thee in thy holy temple.
Men who worship false gods may abandon their loyalty,
but I will offer thee sacrifice with words of praise;
I will pay my vows; victory is the Lord's.

Then the Lord spoke to the fish and it spewed Jonah out on to the dry land.

The word of the Lord came to Jonah a second time: 'Go to the great city of Nineveh, go now and denounce it in the words I give you.' Jonah obeyed at once and went to Nineveh. He began by going a day's journey into the city, a vast city, three days' journey across, and then proclaimed: 'In forty days Nineveh shall be overthrown!' The people of Nineveh believed God's word. They ordered a public fast and put on sackcloth, high and low alike. When the news reached the king of Nineveh he rose from his throne, stripped off his robes of state, put on sackcloth and sat in ashes. Then he had a proclamation made in Nineveh: 'This is a decree of the king and his nobles. No man or beast, herd or flock, is to taste food, to graze or to drink water. They are to clothe themselves in sackcloth and call on God with all their might. Let every man abandon his wicked ways and his habitual violence. It may be that God will repent and turn away from his anger: and so we shall not perish.' God saw what they did, and how they abandoned their wicked ways, and he repented and did not bring upon them the disaster he had threatened.

Jonah was greatly displeased and angry, and he prayed to the Lord: 'This, O Lord, is what I feared when I was in my own country, and to forestall it I tried to escape to Tarshish; I knew that thou art "a god gracious and compassionate, long-suffering and ever constant, and always willing to repent of the disaster." And now, Lord, take my life: I should be better dead than alive.' 'Are you so angry?' said the Lord. Jonah went out and sat down on the east of the city. There he made himself a shelter and sat in its shade, waiting to see what would happen in the city. Then the Lord God ordained that a climbing gourd should grow up over his head to throw its shade over him and relieve his distress, and Jonah was grateful for the gourd. But at dawn the next day God

19

ordained that a worm should attack the gourd, and it withered; and at sunrise God ordained that a scorching wind should blow up from the east. The sun beat down on Jonah's head till he grew faint. Then he prayed for death and said, 'I should be better dead than alive.' At this God said to Jonah, 'Are you so angry over the gourd?' 'Yes,' he answered, 'mortally angry.' The Lord said, 'You are sorry for the gourd, though you did not have the trouble of growing it, a plant which came up in a night and withered in a night. And should not I be sorry for the great city of Nineveh, with its hundred and twenty thousand who cannot tell their right hand from their left, and cattle without number?'

INDUCTIVE QUESTIONS

Here are some basic inductive questions for the Book of Jonah:

1. **What kind** of writing is it? (Story, poetry, or letter?) Is a writer using an "I and you" framework (as in Paul's letters) or is the passage presented in the third person—a "he and they" frame of reference?

(Clue: In Jonah, we have a straightforward story narrated in the third person. Neither the teller of the story, nor his specific historical audience are referred to or directly implicit in the text, as they are in much of the New Testament, and in other Old Testament prophets. Jonah begins with no introductions, settings, or explanations, but simply begins dramatically with "The word of the Lord came to Jonah. . . ." and plunges into the action.) Make other observations about the kind of writing you see here, and jot them down on your paper.

2. **What parts** can you divide the book into? Draw lines between your major divisions right on the page.

(Clue: How do you decide on major divisions? See if your **where, what's happening,** and **when** questions will help you decide. In a story, one way to make divisions is to think of it in scenes. Try dividing the Book of Jonah into scenes.)

3. Give a brief **title** to each part. This will help you concentrate and give you a handy outline.

Now you are ready to begin your careful study of each part. Simply proceed section by section, using questions 4 through 12 as idea-starters for each section, to form your own good observations and further questions. (Some questions will apply more than others to each section.)

4. **Who** are the main characters? Circle them in each section. (They will change from section to section.) Who or what is this story mainly about?

5. **What's happening?** In the margin beside each paragraph, jot down in a sentence or two the main action.

6. **How do characters feel? Why** questions often look at motives. For example, whose idea is it to throw Jonah overboard? What is the motive? How does Jonah feel in his prayer? List other characters and clues about motives. Why does Jonah say that he fled in the first place?

7. **What is contrasted?** List as many examples of people, actions, ideas, attitudes, or things that are contrasted as you can find, moving part by part.

(Clue: For example, how are the sailors contrasted to Jonah? The fish to the worm? What ideas does Jonah contrast in his prayer? You'll find many more contrasts.)

8. **What (or who) causes something else to happen?** You might use arrows to connect as many cause-effect relationships as you can find. For example, what causes the storm, and what effects does the storm have, and what actions are taken because of that? Again, use this question in each part.

9. **What is repeated?** For example, trace the word *presence* or *presence of the Lord*. Where do you find it again after v. 1? Define the phrase from the context. What other kinds of repetition do you observe?

10. **What actions or thoughts are implicity balanced or**

connected? For example, Jonah leaves God's presence in v.
1. Pinpoint the action that brings him back to God. Several
times, people ask mercy at different points. Who are they
and what happens? Is this pattern important? Another "pair"
of actions is that both the sailors and Jonah turn to God with
vows and sacrifices, in parts two and three. Compare this
"pair" of actions. Another "pair" is the lesson of the whale,
and the lesson of the worm. Look further to see. You will find
comparisons within each part, and *between* parts. Note
these observations on paper.

11. **How are things named or described?** Study word
choices. For example, list all the phrases in Jonah's prayer
that describe where he *is,* or *was:* the *belly of Sheol,* etc. . . .
See how these relate. What does God compare the gourd to?

12. **What progression of thought do you see?** In a narrative or story, progression or development usually comes
through the main character. So as you go section by section,
list all you can observe from the text about Jonah. Now,
what conclusions can you draw about Jonah and his relationship to God?

*After you have used questions 4-12 to explore each sec-
tion in turn, you are ready to move toward summary and
application of the whole book.*

13. From what you have learned about God in this whole
story, and from what you have discovered about His purpose for Jonah, and for Nineveh, **what general statement
would you make** about the meaning of this book?

14. **How does the whole story and its meaning apply to
our world and to your life?** What application does God
give? Put God's last speech into your own words.

Now, you really went through Jonah quickly, and barely
skimmed the surface. But you took a first pass at inductive
study. You did it!

If you worked through the exercise and wrote out your answers, you're ready to read on. If you haven't done the exercise yet, you'll find that our next few chapters will make a lot more sense *after* you've had to stare at your "fish" for a while first.

REVIEW AND EVALUATION OF SAMPLE STUDY

- What facts did you learn about Jonah's story that you didn't know before?
  Part of this will depend on whether you've ever read this book before as a whole. Your new discoveries of fact may be minor things, or they may seem very important. But remember—in inductive study, first you find all the clues, then you see ways to relate them, *then* you judge their importance, when you find how the details fit. (For example, perhaps before you looked closely at this book, you would have thought the big fish was much much more important than that little worm. . . .)

Here are some illustrations of new discoveries some teachers have found in their first study of Jonah:

- — It doesn't say it was a whale. People just assume that.
- — The sailors, even though they didn't believe in God, assumed the storm was a punishment for a bad deed.
- — Their answer was to pray to every god anybody knew, and hope to hit the right one. It's ironic that it was a superstitious, pagan captain who woke Jonah up and insisted that he pray to his God.
- — God uses two animal object lessons in Jonah: one using the fish, the other using the worm. These two animals seem to be paired in some way, and stand at the beginning and the end of the book.
- — We can see this story in two big "parts," or in four

smaller ones. But it's all *one* story, about *one* theme.
— Your discoveries

- What change or clarification has occurred in your understanding of the Jonah story as a result of learning new facts or new relationships?
- Why is it just as important to know the part we learn in chapter 4, as it is to know the famous fish episode of chapter 1? How do these parts fit together to show us *two* ways in which Jonah missed God's main idea about Nineveh? How do these two parts, together, add up to the "whole story" that you don't get just from chapter 1?

- Here is how teacher Donald Williams has summarized inductive study into steps: 1) read the whole; 2) state the main point; 3) divide the whole into its natural parts; 4) give a summary and title to each part; 5) analyze each part with inductive questions; 6) look at the relation of parts (contrast, repetition, logic, etc.); 7) generalize and apply. Do you see this general pattern in your sample study?

Generalization and Application?

One of the principles or rules of inductive Bible study is that we do not generalize until we have first studied the "fish" itself closely. Why is that so important if we're to "solve the case" correctly?

Suppose a reader took Jonah 1:1-6 and tried to apply it to his life. How might his application not reflect "the whole story" of the book? How will your application differ if you wait until the whole picture is complete? Which of these applications people might offer would reflect the whole story of Jonah and which ones would not?

1. We must denounce sin.

2. We should dare to find a local situation where someone is disobeying God, such as the X-rated movie downtown, and go tell the offenders that God is displeased and they will be punished unless they repent.

3. When we denounce sin and call for repentance, which God wants us to do, we must do so with a promise of mercy, and with compassion toward the sinner.

4. It's wrong to run away from evil doings, hoping to avoid our responsibility, and it's also wrong to feel angry with sinners.

5. A spirit of vengeance is never a proper attitude when God carries out His punishments, or when He withholds them.

6. It is because God loves sinners more than most of us do that He wants them to be saved from destruction, while many of us, like Jonah, even when we've known this mercy ourselves, would rather see the threat carried out.

Comment: Application statements 1 and 2 apply only to chapter 1 of Jonah, so they don't catch the whole picture. Application statement 5 applies only to chapter 4 of Jonah, so it too is only part of the story. The other statements are all good ways of stating the whole point of the Book of Jonah.

TEST YOURSELF

• Here are some typical comments you would be likely to hear if you listened in to a wide range of Bible discussion groups any Sunday morning.

All the comments represent "natural" approaches to Bible study. Which contributions would belong in an inductive study and which ones would not? (See answers below.)

TEACHING THE BIBLE FROM THE INSIDE OUT

1. As soon as the passage is read, John says, "Why, that reminds me of what happened to me this week. I didn't submit to the authority of my boss at work, and that's just what this verse is talking about." Yes __ No __
2. "I remember what our pastor back home used to say about this chapter. He taught us that . . ." Yes __ No __
3. "I see three main ideas here. . . ." Yes __ No __
4. "Couldn't you summarize the passage by saying . . ." Yes __ No __
5. "How are the ideas in the first paragraph and the second related?" Yes __ No __
6. "The cross reference in my Bible says to look at Psalm 46: 3 for the same idea." Yes __ No __
7. "This is the same word that's in John 4: 8, where it says. . . ." Yes __ No __
8. "Before we start talking about this passage, we need to be aware that some other denominations use these verses to support their view of baptism." Yes __ No __
9. "The text doesn't use these terms, but isn't this really the same as Gestalt psychology?" Yes __ No __
10. "I think what we ought to do is to go through the passage verse by verse, and see how each verse applies to our lives. After all, application is very important." Yes __ No __
11. "I was reading what Francis Schaefer said about this passage, and he really summed it up for me. He said . . ." Yes __ No __
12. "Let's begin our study by reading the whole passage through, by paragraphs." Yes __ No __

Answers: Only 3, 4, 5 and 12 are inductive contributions. The other comments introduce outside sources, or move to other parts of the Bible, or cannot be discussed without outside knowledge or background the group members do not have.

QUESTIONS, QUESTIONS
Preparing To Lead

". . . here was a man who seemed to be quite as anxious as I, that I should see for myself what he saw."

Let's think about questions. It's clear by now that asking good questions is at the heart of inductive Bible study, and it's the essence of good teaching.

A common misunderstanding about inductive Bible study is that whenever any leader or teacher uses questions to promote discussion, the method is automatically inductive. Not so! There are inductive and deductive questions, and each have their own characteristics. How can you tell inductive questions?

If Professor Agassiz had chosen to *guide* his student in inductive study, (instead of leaving the room!) he would have stood behind his student and said, "Now how are the scales arranged?" "Does the fish have eyelids?" and "Tell

27

me just what the tail looks like." The answers are found in the fish itself.

The student is still a discoverer, because the questions are inductive in nature. They make the student or reader observe the text and draw conclusions. The questions help speed up the observing and relating process and have been planned to reveal the nature of the fish.

If you ask inductive questions about the Book of Jonah, they might be of this kind: "In Jonah's prayer, how does he feel about the events of chapter 1?" "What specific reason does Jonah give to God to explain why he ran away?" "What does God specifically compare the gourd with in 4:10-11?" "Why?"

To judge a teacher, listen to his questions.

AN EXERCISE

Here is an exercise that may help teachers clarify the difference between inductive and deductive questions:

Suppose Mr. Iverson and Mrs. Drury are two teachers in the same Sunday school, teaching the same lesson, on Jonah, to the same age group—sixth grade, let's say.

Mr. Iverson understands how to teach inductively, while Mrs. Drury uses a deductive approach. Below are a few of the questions Mr. Iverson has written down, after his personal inductive study, for teaching his sixth graders. Notice how the questions connect to lead to a discovery by his students. Alongside his questions, you see a few of the deductive questions which Mrs. Drury plans to use.

Do Mrs. Drury's questions link together in a process of discovery? Do they lead the students into more deeply exploring the text itself? That is how you test inductive questions.

Which teacher is "teaching the Bible from the inside out"? Which teacher has the best chance of catching the interest of the sixth graders?

Mr. Iverson's Questions	*Mrs. Drury's Questions*
Introduction: "Today, class, the first part of the story begins as Jonah decided to run away from God. We'll find out first why he wanted to run away and what happened to him next . . ."	*Introduction:* "Today, class, we're going to learn what Jonah learned: that no one can run away from God."
(First, Mr. Iverson has the class read the entire story through.)	*(She tells the story, emphasizing chapters 1-3, and passing over the events of chapter 4. She tells only the part that seems to fit her theme: no one can escape God.)*
"Everybody knows that Jonah was swallowed by a fish. But let's look at exactly what led up to that." (With a series of "Why" questions, he asks several students to piece together the chain of cause and effect that put Jonah at the bottom of the sea.)	"Who was Jonah?" "The great storm on the sea was Jonah's fault. Who can quickly find chapter 1, verse 12 to prove to us that this is true?"
"Look at Jonah's prayer in 2:1-9 and tell us briefly just how he felt. Was he angry? Sorry for himself? Happy? How did you expect him to feel now? Are you surprised?"	"I've selected Jonah's beautiful statement of obedience as our memory verse for today. Let's spend the next few moments memorizing it:
"Have the events of chapter 1 reassured Jonah? Or only terrified him about God?"	'Men who worship false gods may abandon their loyalty but I will offer sacrifices with words of praise; I will pay my vows; victory is the Lord's.' "

Mr. Iverson's Questions	*Mrs. Drury's Questions*
"What is the word of the Lord that comes to Jonah the second time? How is it different from the first time God told Jonah to go to Nineveh? (Asks for comparison with the phrasing of 1:1.) Why might it help Jonah to be told this time that God will give him the words?"	One critic has suggested that the whale is a symbol of redemption, or of Christ. Is there evidence in the story to support that idea?
"What happens when Jonah goes ahead and prophecies at Nineveh? How does Jonah respond to these results? How is his response different from God's feelings about Nineveh?"	Scholars have found evidence that Nineveh was one of the biggest, most advanced and sophisticated cities of its day. How does that help us to understand this story?
"After he goes to Nineveh, and is talking to God in 4:1, Jonah explains to God exactly why he ran away in the beginning. What's really peculiar and surprising about the reason he gives?"	"The moral of the story is: obey God. How do we see that moral expressed in verses 1:1-6?"
"What is the message of the whole book?"	The Book of Jonah was one of the very first books of the Bible ever translated into English so that common people could read it themselves. Why do you think this book was so important and appealing to the common reader four hundred years ago?
"How can we apply this to our daily lives?"	"How can we apply this in our lives?"

30

QUESTIONS CONDENSE THE PROCESS

Whether you try to work out your own set of questions, or whether you use a guide or curriculum, your goal will be the same: to help your students enjoy the same experience of discovering the facts of the passage as you did in your personal study, and to help them form conclusions *themselves* based on those facts.

The most important function of a teacher's guide for good inductive Bible study is to supply you with good questions.

Inductive teaching depends not so much on what is *in* the teacher's guide, as how you prepare and present it. The discovery process will be limited to somewhere between 30 and 60 minutes. So your function will be to condense the process *you* followed in personal study, and still follow the inductive scheme. Your answer to the time problem will *not* be to simply deliver the results or conclusions you drew and cite a few verses to support it.

For example, if you are sensitive to inductive process, you would never start a lesson by stating your conclusion, such as, "Today, class, we're going to see how Jonah finds out that he cannot run away from God." That's a deductive approach (and besides, it's not the main point of the Book of Jonah!).

An inductive introduction to Jonah would be something more like this: "Today class, we're going to see what happens when Jonah decides to run away from a job God gave him."

It is crucial that students discover for themselves, using their eyes, their brains, and the Bible. They need to see from their own experience that they can understand what the Bible says and that they do not need an expert coming between them and God's Word. The only way they can

31

learn this is to be put into the laboratory with the fish—no amount of lecture will do it.

A Test

The best test to apply to a question, to see if it's inductive, is to ask how it will work for the group. Nobody could ever give you a pat list of inductive or deductive questions. Here's why.

Whether a question is inductive can depend on what the book or passage is. Questions like "Who was this first written to?" could stimulate lots of inductive observations in a letter of Paul, but would be a deductive question when asked about Jonah: you could only answer it by looking "outside" the text.

Whether a question is inductive can also depend on how you answer it. Suppose you ask, "What sort of city was Nineveh?" Students could grab first for the Bible encyclopedia or dictionary, or you could ask them simply to see how much they could learn about Nineveh from the book itself. (An amazing number of good inferences about Nineveh's social structure, size, population, and sophistication *can* be made, just by poring over the text and looking attentively.) The question itself was neither inductive nor deductive.

Are all inductive questions good ones for teaching? Certainly there are bad, boring inductive questions, just as there are bad, boring deductive ones! A teacher could bore a class to tears by asking only dry, unrelated fact questions that are too simple; yet each question might be inductive in the sense that you can answer it by looking in the Bible!

Good inductive questions lead to a path of discovery and learning by the students themselves. Keep asking, How do my questions *work?* Do they lead into the text and show relationships?

HOW CAN I PREPARE TO LEAD A CLASS INDUCTIVELY?

Here's how any teacher, using any curriculum, can begin using the basic concept of inductive study in preparing a lesson.

- Whether you're a greenhorn teacher or a pro, whether you're using curriculum material, a discussion guide, or are making up your own questions, your first step in any preparation is always to read the Bible passage the group is going to study. Break the old habit of saying, "I'd better read the teacher's guide first, so I'll know what to look for in the Bible passage." And never say, "Oh that story. I don't need to read it again—I already know it." If a lesson plan refers you only to a few verses—**read them in context.**
- After you have followed the process of observation, understanding, application in your personal study (review chapter 2, pp. 15-27), think through ways to make the lesson a discovery process for your students as well.
- Each week, use a few of the specific reading skills that characterize inductive study with your students. (For instance, one week you might have them look for contrasts. Another time, you might have them look for all the examples of cause-effect relationships. Still another time, you might ask the class to tell you everything that happened in a narrative passage, in the order in which it occurred.)
- Once you have studied the passage on your own, see what additional insights your teacher's quarterly can give you. Spend a little time seeing how your personal study and the teaching material fit together, so that you have a unified lesson that clearly moves to the main point of the Bible passage.
- Make sure each student has a Bible under his nose, preferably in a readable, modern translation.

Inductive study is an ideal approach for the new Sunday school teacher who may be just one week ahead of his students. The teacher is not functioning like a great Bible encyclopedia.

—Marilyn Kunz

There isn't another book in the world that's been more misquoted, regardless of context or purpose or reference, than the Bible. That's one reason inductive principles are so important.

—Catherine Schell

SUNDAY SHOES
Leading Inductive Groups

"Take this fish," said he, "and look at it: we call it a Haemulon; by and by I will ask you what you have seen."
In ten minutes I had seen all that could be seen in that fish, and started in search of the professor, who had, however, left the museum. . . .

When you step into your Sunday shoes next week, how are you going to apply what you've learned about inductive Bible study? Should you throw away your teacher's guide? Bring a fish to class with you? Say nothing? Or, following Professor Agassiz, just give your students each a Bible and leave the room? Well, you probably won't do any of these! So let's look further.

In the next section, our four contributing teachers give their insights on questions about leadership.

TEACHING THE BIBLE FROM THE INSIDE OUT

WHAT IS THE LEADER'S ROLE IN INDUCTIVE BIBLE STUDY?
Don Williams:

The key here is *attitude.* Most of us came through a church system and a school system in which teachers were authority figures. Students (whether children or adults) looked up to teachers and depended on them to give the "right" answers.

As we begin teaching inductive study, our job is to demonstrate, not just say, that all of us in the group are accountable to the Bible passage we are studying. We point our students back to the text, and to each other's insights on the text, instead of answering questions ourselves.

That takes real discipline on our parts!

The more advanced and mature you are as a Bible student, the more care it will take on your part to resist that old temptation to lead others with too heavy a hand. I know. Sometimes, since I do have a Ph.D in Biblical study, and teach at a seminary, I find people in a class looking to me for approval of their right answers. I need to find ways to set them free, and direct them back into the text.

One simple way you can reinforce the idea in your meeting is to sit in a circle with your class. Inductive Bible study is much better represented by a circle of chairs than by a lectern or desk.

Another method I've found works is to divide a class into small groups, each to study a paragraph, and then I leave them on their own for a time. I'm not there to hear their right answers. This helps them work as a team, and forces them not to treat the leader as an authority.

As teachers, we need to understand authority as service. The way I serve your Christian maturity is by giving you tools and setting you free to use them.

WHOSE GROUP IS IT?
Catherine Schell:

In a discussion overly dominated by the teacher, the group comments could be pictured as a fan. The teacher asks every question, solicits every reply, and comments on every contribution.

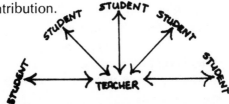

Your goal is to change this discussion pattern to one of a many-sided star. In this pattern, group members respond to each other, or question each other's insights; they observe and clarify without the teacher interfering in the process.

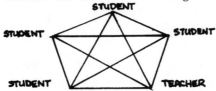

For a week or two, observe the discussion pattern of your group. Do you see some tendencies toward the fan picture? If so, use some of the following techniques to help change the pattern:

- Be sure *you* are not answering others' questions. Insist the students work out the problem together, from their observations of the text and their own insights. Often, this means answering a question with a question.
- Never answer your own questions. If there is no reply to a question, after you have waited, either rephrase the question in another way, or suggest that the group come back to that one later.
- Don't be satisfied with one answer to a question, even if you consider it a good one. Often you can ask

another group member, "Don, do you agree with what Mary said?" or, "Helen, do you see anything else in the passage?" Look around the circle, catching the eye of one or more members. You can tell who's got a thought. It won't be many weeks before the students will start commenting on each other's comments without any cues from you at all.

- Don't "reward" answers you approve of ("That's very good, Mary." "That was just what I was looking for, Tom.") If you compliment a good, rich answer, you're indirectly saying, "And that's the end of that discussion."
- Give people time to think. Don't be afraid of a little silence.

WHAT ABOUT WRONG ANSWERS?
Marilyn Kunz:

You'll find a group is self-corrective. Very often, when someone makes a wild comment, someone will say, "Boy, I don't know where you got that. Here's what I see in the passage . . ." so the group corrects itself.

Remember, an inductive approach to Scripture is different than a bull session approach in which anything goes and the emphasis is on "what I feel about these ideas," or just "my opinions in general," rather than what the passage means. Too many church Bible studies which are not designed with inductive discipline deteriorate into vague disputes about each other's ideas, or doctrines, or differing commentators, or political vagaries, rather than mutual close reading of the passage and the generalizations it will clearly support.

Suppose some people are brainstorming a passage, especially if they are new to the Scripture, and suppose some of the things they seem to discover appear to be correct in the light of the passage, but you know they do not fit into the teaching of Scripture as a whole.

First, try to pin down the things that can be corrected from the passage. Out of ten incorrect things, perhaps two are clearly related to the point of this Scripture passage. Zero in on those two items. Here you can see one of the advantages of limiting yourself to one passage. Say, "John, you commented thus and so. Could you back up your conclusions from what we have in today's study? Where do you see _____ ? Could you show us the verses that suggest this idea to you?"

Sometimes, when John looks at the verses, he will realize he hadn't read them correctly the first time, and he will correct himself. Sometimes, you'll have to ask a couple of other questions to get him to see the problem, or you may be able to make a few comments (as a last resort) that will put the verses in the context of the whole chapter.

Sometimes, though, some of the comments that worry you because you know they're incorrect are not dealt with in the passage you're studying. John has no basis for seeing his error. If you feel the point is significant, you can do one of two things: either make a note to be sure to discuss it later, when a later passage bears on the point, or else simply acknowledge that you're dropping the inductive process for a moment to give some direct comment. There is a place for this within an inductive study, when a wrong comment really requires a correction.

But allowing the group, as much as possible, to be self-corrective is far better than to be constantly evaluating and saying, "Oh, John, that's not right," and "Mary, that's a wrong interpretation of the passage," and then explaining in great detail what you know. There's enough to learn in any new section that you must concentrate on the passage. As long as your overall purpose is to build a solid sense of how to move from evidence to conclusions, you can trust people's continued exposure to God's Word to enlighten and correct the fine points over the course of time.

WHAT ABOUT THE PROBLEM TALKER?
Marilyn Kunz:

Suppose you have a class member who has some decided doctrinal problems, either in form of pet theories he keeps insisting on in class or in loaded questions he keeps bringing up, whether or not they reflect the main point of the lesson.

When this happens, do not try to work out the tangents with the group (unless the whole group is hung up on the point). You'll invite class boredom or even resentment if you permit a single person's side issues to dominate.

Whether you're a Sunday school teacher or a discussion leader in a home study, you have to assume you will be investing some time beyond the hour once a week in the lives of your group members. This situation calls for some of that extra time. After class, or in a phone conversation, suggest getting together. Say, "Bill, I know you're really interested in—. Could we get together for an hour this week and talk about that some more?"

If the person has a soapbox problem, your job will first be to listen to what he has to say and try to understand why this particular issue is important to him. You might want to look at some Scripture passages with him—as co-learners, not trying to club each other over the head with your favorite verses, but trying to see that issue in perspective.

Then you can share with him the goals of inductive study (self discovery, understanding the main point of a passage, etc.), perhaps asking him to skim through this book for an overview. In most cases, you will be able to turn a thorn in your flesh into a valuable ally, once he knows he's not being ignored and once his effort is personally solicited to help class stay with the main discussion.

HOW DO I HANDLE CONFLICTS?
Marilyn Kunz:

Suppose you are reading a passage that has several possible interpretations. A person who is new to Bible study will tend to think, "There must be just one right answer." If it does not appear simple, he may distrust his ability to read.

This is the time when the "expert," who knows the church has not reached one conclusion over the centuries, can point out the three or four possible ideas that come from the passage. If your group has drawn more than one idea from a passage, and the implications conflict, you might say, "What the church has not solved in several thousand years, we aren't going to settle in an hour. Our particular denomination (if yours is a church group) tends to feel that this view is most acceptable."

If your denomination does not have a position on that point, you can simply describe the differing views and say, "Isn't it interesting that in our own group, we have reflected the very same differences that the church has struggled with for centuries."

POINTERS ON LEADING INDUCTIVE STUDY WITH ADULTS
Catherine Schell:

If you teach adults, all of the pointers in the preceding part of this chapter will be helpful to you. But let's take a look at the specific techniques you might use as you begin inductive study with an adult class for the first time.

If you have a class of twenty people or more, for instance, try dividing them into groups of two or three people by forming small buzz groups right where they're seated. Then assign each group a paragraph of the Bible passage you're studying that week. (Two or three small groups might be studying the same paragraph.) Then give each group one to three inductive questions on their paragraph (having, of course, written these out ahead of time). Give the groups five to ten minutes to study and discover what their paragraph said.

When you call the whole group back together, move through the passage, having one member of each group report their findings. After this process, you might summarize the whole passage again and comment or lecture briefly, then look to the whole group for suggested applications.

If you have ten or fewer class members, try keeping the group together and move through the passage paragraph by paragraph (not verse by verse), asking the inductive questions yourself. Give them time to think about the questions, and don't be afraid of silences—people need time to think. Watch people's eyes and call on quiet ones who are probably ready to contribute but can't quite muster up the courage.

When the inductive approach is new to an adult group, it can be a slow, miserable time for the first few weeks. But if you're positive and accepting, and keep turning people back to Scripture, expecting them to discover things for themselves, they soon begin to respond.

Of course, your most important contribution will be good study and discussion questions to help the people dig into the passage and to share with the group. Good questions are the responsibility of the leader and the curriculum or study guide. If you choose material that is based on an inductive approach and ask questions that help students find out what is in Scripture, you're well on your way to a successful inductive Bible study.

As soon as we use the word "leader," we bring to mind a mental picture of one person standing in front of others sharing the truth he has. What I've really enjoyed about inductive Bible study is that I don't even have to attempt to play that role. In inductive study, you still have a leader. The leader is just operating under a different set of principles.

–Norman Bell

In inductive study, the discussion is going with the Scripture. If the Scripture goes somewhere, then the discussion goes somewhere. It's the bull session approach to the Bible that goes nowhere, where people are arguing pro and con about predestination and so forth. That's the kind of discussion that goes nowhere.

–Marilyn Kunz

If I give people an authoritative answer, then their confidence is vested in me rather than in the Scriptures. And usually, they won't remember three weeks later what my great answer was; they will only remember that I had a great answer.

–Marilyn Kunz

THE BIBLE IS IN!
WITH TEENS
Insights for High School Teachers

There's an old story about a professor who asked a physics student, "Do you know what electricity is?"

The student thought a moment. Finally he said, "I knew, but I forgot."

The professor smote his forehead. "Oh, no!" he said, "the only man who ever understood electricity, and he forgot!"

If you've ever taught high school students, maybe you know some young people who "knew, but they forgot" something we wanted them to learn. How many persons who finish ten or twelve years of Sunday school today could quickly answer these questions:

Who lived first, Moses or Abraham?

What happened at the first Passover?

Name three people who saw Jesus after He
rose from the dead.
What is the main message of any one of Paul's
letters you may know?

The trouble is, if we've ever really known something, we couldn't have forgotten. How did adolescents and young adults *master* something they once were taught?

Let's look at another problem. How many young people have never been able to establish habits of personal Bible study? How many are struggling with doubts, or trying to develop an adult faith on the basis of lots of bull sessions and very little real understanding of what the Bible says? Can they push beyond a child's acquaintance with a few isolated, simplified stories and a collection of memorized verses?

Here is how one high school teacher we'll call Mrs. James described her experience in turning some ordinary, ho-hum high school Bible students into young people alive to the Word.

MRS. JAMES' STORY:

I didn't think I had much to lose in trying some inductive methods with my class. In fact, I'd been wondering, at the time I learned about inductive Bible study, whether I should quit. Maybe what my class needed was some dynamo— somebody more glamorous or younger than me. Oh, my students were good kids. They were committed to the faith, and respectful toward me, most of the time. But they didn't have the spark.

I decided to give it one more try—with an inductive experiment. One week, I told them we were trying something new. I said, "Who's ever heard of Amos?"

"Amos who?"

"The prophet Amos," I said.

"Oh—you mean in the Bible? Yeah, I guess I've heard of him."

Sally, the minister's daughter, was quickly rehearsing her books of the Bible. "Comes right after Joel," she said.

"Let's take the next seven weeks and give them to Amos," I suggested. "Haven't you ever wondered what some of these books you hardly ever heard of are doing in the Bible? Let's just figure out what one book we don't know is all about—what it has to say."

I could see they weren't ready for this. But I said, "This week—we start on Amos, on our own." I had made a copy of the book, from a large print Bible, for each of my eight students, and handed them these manuscripts.

First, we read it all the way through, rapidly, and then looked at the major parts. That was all we got done the first week. But already they were intrigued. This *was* something new.

The next week, everybody was there. And over the next few weeks, there was a definite change in that group. We dug. We compared. We used atlases and maps. We marked up Bible parts, noted repeated patterns, wrote questions, talked, and used pencils. We studied Amos inductively.

We looked at this word *justice* that keeps pounding through the book. We watched what Amos meant by it. We asked ourselves, "Who is he talking to?" "Does Amos come on like a radical, or wild man?" "How does he see himself?" We looked at how he contrasts justice with propriety or social custom. We looked at what God may mean in the line, "O Israel, you love to do what is proper!"

The class role-played the dramatic scene in Amos, where he has a run-in with the high priest who tells him, "Go back to the hills and don't come around here!" And we looked at this Old Testament God who is both just and merciful.

As we dug, we found the balance and the power of the whole book. We felt we understood why this particular book has a place in the Bible. Result? They owned Amos. I felt they would never forget it. It wasn't magic. But it was involvement.

"Okay," I said seven weeks later when the study was ending, "now you're going to turn around and do Amos, as team teachers, to a class of junior highs—Mrs. Dawson's class. She's asked us what all the excitement is about. How about showing them?"

"Oh, no," said Tom. "My brother's in there. You can't teach him anything." The class chuckled. But I insisted. So, we held some strategy meetings. The question was, how do you get ninth graders into the Bible—from the inside out? "We've got to use a game," said Tom. "My brother doesn't learn too well unless he's *moving* with it. You have to give him a new idea by setting it up so he thinks it's *his* idea." We came up with two games. I find a game works better than ten explanations, to help show inductive goals, and build some curiosity and enthusiasm.

Game 1 - *Who Took My Orange?* The idea is to *DO* the inductive idea before you explain it. You explain induction, inductively! In this game, you start with a bowl or basket or bag of oranges—one for each student. You say to the class, "These are all oranges—all pretty much the same, right?"

"Right," they say.

"Okay, each person take one orange. Now I'll give you two minutes to study your own particular individual orange. Look at the bumps, the dents, the spots, the special coloring; study that thing carefully. Then we're going to put them all back in the basket."

They study. For two minutes, each kid gets involved—very involved—with the clues and details that make that orange what it is. Then, you collect the oranges, mix them up in the basket, spread them out, and then give each person a chance to reclaim "his orange."

They are amazed to see that a student can easily pick out the particular orange he studied. He sees how it's different from all the rest.

Now ask them what they have discovered from this game and how it might relate to studying a book of the Bible. When they tell you, you reply that they've learned one very basic thing—about Bible study that's exciting, because it stays with you. Each study becomes much more than just "the same old bag of oranges."

Game 2 - *Telephone.* Remember the old parlor game called Telephone? The group sits in a circle. You announce that this is a relay message on a human telephone. You will whisper a one-sentence message to the first member of the group. He whispers it to his neighbor one time (no repeats) as clearly as he can; that neighbor relays it to his neighbor, and so on around the circle. The last person reports out loud the message that he heard. It's always a good laugh to see how the message has changed.

Now you place a Bible in the center of the circle and say, "Now suppose the original message I gave John had been a report of something that's in the Bible. How has this game related to ways of learning about the Bible?

When they tell you, you point out that they've discovered one other very basic reason we do inductive Bible study—that the only valid source of what the Bible teaches is the Bible itself. Otherwise, the message gets fuzzy and confused.

On the board, draw a circle of believers, and the Bible in the center. Draw lines from each believer to the center, so that it makes a wheel design. Explain that the strength of the wheel (the body of believers) depends on the spokes of each person's direct connection with Jesus Christ as He is revealed in the Bible.

Say that reading the Bible involves some skills of study—not just a quick pass at some verses now and then, but a learning how to learn. Your spoke of the wheel is permanent, though your neighbors in the circle change and vary, and see things differently. Explain that even your greatest teacher, or the greatest Bible scholar you'll ever know, is still only one of your helping neighbors, *not* the center of the wheel.

Once you've introduced the idea, with a game, simply plunge into inductive study, using the techniques you find described in this book. Make it challenging and active and you'll find the young people responding.

There are several other tips I learned about inductive teaching for high school people. Here they are:

- Pre-tests and post-tests are popular. Let the students make up pre-tests and post-tests. Make the tests ''open book'' (using Bibles to answer inductive questions), and keep the tone light and fun, not heavy-handed.
- Challenge, challenge! Teens are more put off by questions that are too simple, or do not lead to new thought, than they are by challenging questions that require some real digging and thinking.
- Adolescents are more ready than perhaps any other age group to ask, ''Is anybody doing what we say we're supposed to be doing?'' None of our Sunday school classes need effective, no-nonsense application times more than adolescents do. (See Chapter 7 on application for more specific help.)

   In addition, when teaching adolescents, rely on your teacher's guide as well as your own ideas for roleplay, skits, finishing the story, or creative writing ideas to involve students in expressive learning.
- All of the reasons for using the overhead projector for children (see p. 53) apply to teens, too.

TEACHING THE BIBLE FROM THE INSIDE OUT

Anyone who works with adolescents knows that this age group has a deep capacity for both doubt, or questions, and for enthusiasm and commitment. Perhaps when you try some of the basic discovery techniques that inductive study uses, you'll know the thrill, when that bell or chime marks the end of your Sunday school hour, of hearing your students say, "Oh, shucks, Mrs. James, do we have to stop now?"

I've heard that complaint myself, several times, and believe me, it's a complaint I can take!

It seems you have to be such a super expert in this world to find out something that others haven't learned. In the sciences, post-doctoral work barely gets you into areas where others haven't been. So little seems left to discover in this world. If we can help people to get the thrill of discovery, it's the kind of thing that will inspire a person to move on.

–Norman Bell

For whom is the Bible intended? Were the first-century gnostics correct that it was all an inside secret message for a select few?

–Marilyn Kunz

ADVENTURES WITH KIDS
*Third Grade Through Eighth Grade**

There was a near silence in our junior church as twenty kids read to themselves from a huge screen the large-print, dramatic story found in Mark 8: 22-26. Some moved their lips, or read it to their neighbors, quietly.

"Hey!" said Jimmy, age nine, who seemed to finish first. "You know what? Jesus is healing this blind guy, but look at that—he had to try two times!" He frowned and stood up in his pew. The projector hummed in the dark as the other kids took a moment to see what the big, black words said, and hear what Jimmy had said.

It was junior church and my twenty juniors were involved—really involved—in inductive Bible study.

I asked Jimmy to take the pointer and show where he got that from the story. He did this.

* Chapter based on interviews with consulting teacher Norman Bell.

51

"That's funny," Sarah continued. "I always thought if Jesus was going to heal someone, He could do it on the first try."

"You've got some good observations there," I said, not commenting further just yet. "What do you see here, Mark?"

"Jesus uses some spit to do this," Mark said. "Wow! I never heard of that before."

"How do you know that?" says Sarah.

"Look at verse 23, where it says *spat*. That means he spitted, doesn't it?"

"That's right, Mark." "Mary, what do you see?"

"Jesus keeps this a secret," Mary said.

"How do you know?" Mark asks.

"Look at verse 26. Jesus sent him straight home. He told the man not to go back to the village."

"Good observation," I said. "Now look at verse 23."

"Yeah," said Mark, "it looks like Jesus is making sure he gets out of the village and away from the crowd before he even starts to heal the man," said Jimmy.

"That's kind of strange," said Mary. She tends to grasp bigger ideas, to fit things together into a speculation. "I always thought Jesus wanted to do His miracles in order to get people curious so they would notice Him and listen to Him. But in this story, that must not be what He wants. . . ."

Would you like to see young people this involved in really looking at the Bible "from the inside out"? I find I can use a very open kind of inductive Bible study with children as young as third or fourth grade—as soon as they can read pretty well. I've used it in settings from junior church to regular Sunday school classes. For me, inductive study works—or rather, I should say—for *us,* it works. The kids are excited.

When you ask kids, "What do you see here?" paragraph

by paragraph, one small story at a time, they really look and they really see. They're not as self-conscious as adults and I find they're not as worried about showing their ignorance or saying wrong things. They catch on very quickly to the idea of building what they say from the text.

Let me share some tips I think are important to help a teacher use the good features of inductive study with children.

As a professor and university researcher in educational psychology, I know some of the things teachers often worry about with kids in reading the Bible. *Can* they read it? Does the Bible seem strange and out of date to them? Can they really grasp concepts? Don't they need a lot of guidance? Here are some of the solutions I've found from experience:

First, think about your students as readers. Have faith in them. Read *naturally* as a class. The verse by verse round robin reading of stories from a hodge-podge of different Bibles, each in tiny print, is a fact of life in many Sunday schools. This way of involving children, in my opinion, doesn't give them the best chance to understand.

Have them read in paragraphs, not verse by verse. It's more important to follow a whole thought than to make sure each child reads "the same amount."

Second, it's much better to let children read a passage through silently and then paraphrase, rather than to expect clear oral reading of a strange passage the first time. Have them read a whole unit before you look at the parts. Kids, like adults, want to see the whole shape. Fragmented presentation is frustrating to them.

Try hard to get printed material that's *big*. Children need big print; they can't get motivated to tackle the dense print in small Bibles, and time is wasted as they hunt for verses. My own favorite method is the overhead projector. It dramatizes that the Bible is the "big cheese," not me. Even when they no longer *need* such big print, it still helps them.

With a little practice, you can also project a sheet on which you can write with a grease pencil, right before their very eyes, to record their comments or questions, or to mark words or underline what they point out. This creates group feeling, and the children feel what *they* say is new, and important, because the teacher is writing it down! What a switch—the teacher takes notes on what *I* said!

As you use questions with the overhead projector, you can snap the story on and off. Ask a question. Get an answer. To check it, flip the overhead back on. Dramatically and simply, the young people see that the answers are in the Bible, not in the teacher. They grasp the inductive idea.

Letting children use a stick pointer can help them get up on their chairs and notice specific words or parts of the text, or back up their comments, without my repeating directions or hearing voices say, "Where are we? Which verse?" All these techniques, and lots more that you can think up, can emphasize the group feeling that inductive study builds.

Paraphrasing is an important skill children can develop. "Put it in your own words," the teacher says, and they do. Children beyond third grade can hold a story sequence in order in their minds and think back over it. The results are delightful, often accurate, and sometimes enlighten me as to how a child has misconceived something. If something is said wrong, the group often corrects it. Or you can ask for another child's summary. This gives review in a fresh way and helps the slower child assimilate. A quick role play can be another effective review.

Never, never answer your own question or tell someone outright, "No, that's wrong." If a question is unanswered, *wait.* Give them time. Too many teachers jump into every empty space. If there's still no answer, rephrase the question. Or go on, and come back to the hard one later.

Never introduce abstractions from outside the passage. Children perceive concepts gradually. Remember the limits.

They're in what Piaget calls the "concrete-operational" phase of intellectual development, in the upper elementary grades. They need to observe patterns closely and specifically before they can generalize. This is why the scheme and spirit of inductive study—observations before relationships before generalizations—helps children so much. It fits the way their minds work.

I know it takes a bit of nerve, and a bit of faith, to start kids out on an inductive Bible study. They may not respond right away. You have to give it some time. It's not a panacea—and teaching junior church isn't a teacher's dreamland, either. I have to keep things moving 'til I hear the organ upstairs, and sometimes that's a challenge. You don't get rid of all the discipline problems overnight, or miraculously cure children of boredom. But in my experience, in inductive study, more children feel more involved than they do in many other ways I know to teach.

Adventure is a key word in childhood. So is "I can do it myself." Adventure and self-reliance are feelings built into inductive Bible study. Too many of their teachers and schoolbook texts take the joy and meaning out of learning by making it dry, boring memory work and listening. So let them be the investigators. I think you may have some fresh, adventurous young people on your hands.

Personally, even though I'm a university professor and have been teaching kids, and adults, and college students for years, I keep finding that the children's naturally direct, immediate approach to things, and their new insights make them naturals for inductive study. What they see is often inspiring—and it often teaches me something about the mind of Christ.

LIVING PROOF
Applying Inductive Study

Jesus insists that doing His word is the only test there is of whether we have understood and accepted it. He was never satisfied with merely verbal or mental learning.

In the following sections, our contributing teachers discuss how to help your students draw correct applications.

A GOOD APPLICATION APPLIES THE MAIN POINT
Catherine Schell:

Our applications need to come from the principles we have discovered in the passage. We can miss the mark with tiny, spiritualized points that come from a sort of odd interpretation of only one phrase. I think the Holy Spirit does speak to people through a phrase of Scripture and that God puts up with a lot of our oddball ideas because He's kind and gracious. He recognizes that we're children at times.

But what I'm out for as a Sunday school teacher is to help people to stop being children and grow up in their faith. Therefore, what I'm aiming for is to help them begin to apply the principles they have found by their observations and careful study.

For example, in Luke 15, Jesus tells three stories in order to answer the Pharisees' objection to His eating with people they call "sinners"—tax collectors and the like. These three parables are the lost sheep, the lost coin, and then the story we call the prodigal son.

In the story about the woman who loses the coin, she sweeps the house and searches diligently for her coin. Then she rejoices with her neighbors when she finds it. The point Jesus makes is that there is just such rejoicing in heaven when one sinner repents.

Now suppose someone reading the story says, "Oh boy, this really speaks to me about the fact that I'm not a very good housekeeper. She found the coin because she swept her house diligently."

As the leader of the group, what are you going to say about this person's response? She may be making a valid point about being a poor housekeeper, and perhaps the Holy Spirit is telling her that she ought to do better at it. But that's not really the point of this parable.

If I were leading the group, I wouldn't say, "Oh, but that's not the point here." I would just say, "That's interesting. It might be a good idea to have a cleaner house, if that's what the Lord is talking to you about. But what point is Jesus making here? Do you see anything further? How does this story tie in with the one before it? What do you see in common here? What is lost? What is found? What is the reaction of the finder?"

So I would lead the group back into the passage to see the major point Jesus is making. In Luke 15, that main point certainly is: What kind of attitude do we have toward people who are in the category of "sinner"? Are we like the Pharisee who is too proud to share God's attitude toward the tax collector, or are we like the father who welcomes his son back when the lost is found? Or do we see ourselves as the good son who has done all the right things but who is still alienated from his father in his heart?

My goal as leader is to help the group make an application that comes from the main point of the study.

APPLICATION IS A LAST STEP
Marilyn Kunz:

One problem teachers may have with the inductive method is helping the group save application and life response for the last step. In the observation stage, we do not have enough information to make application, and any application remark, even if it is correct and good, is really a tangent that you hope you can prevent the group from following until later. The old habit of moving verse by verse in our study is part of the problem, many times. We apply before we have grasped the whole picture.

In the story of the lost coin, for example, if we move verse by verse, applying as we go, the housework application might strike many of the group members as apt, original, and insightful, when in fact, it entirely misses Jesus' point in telling the story.

Save application and life response for the last step. The result will be more fresh, incisive, and more spiritually perceptive responses because the group's comments will be drawn from a thorough grasp of the chapter or passage.

In Sunday school settings, too often application and life response are not a separate step at all, or else get squeezed into the last three minutes of the session. Part of your job as teacher is to plan your time carefully so that you deliberately give perhaps as much as a third of your total time to summary, questions of application, and life response.

APPLICATION AS BEHAVIORAL OBJECTIVES
Norman Bell:

Application is the key to the whole thing in inductive Bible study. To gain knowledge and not apply it to your life is senseless.

In working with high school and college students, we've helped them set behavioral objectives. For instance, we give them a card that reads, "On the basis of what I've learned today, I'm going to _____." And they fill in the blanks. We tell them to to put the card away and then bring it out and check their progress every now and then.

Another idea we've used is a memo "from me to me." Each student writes out what he's going to do because of what he's learned that day. Then he seals the note in an envelope. We collect the memos and save them for a month. When we return the goal statements, the students evaluate their progress.

THE TEACHER IS THE LESSON
Marilyn Kunz:

In a real sense, when it comes to application, the teacher is the lesson. Any Bible study material, whether it's Sunday school curriculum or a discussion guide, is going to have to be somewhat general in its suggestions for application. After all, that printed material reaches a wide audience of varied ages, nationalities, and life-styles.

But you as teacher or leader know your group and can be sensitive to the most appropriate ways to apply the Bible passage you have studied.

People learn best by example. The best way to encourage

your students to make personal application is to briefly share a recent situation from your own life in which this lesson truth comes home to you.

But never forget that Christianity is not just what we say. Don't let your students assume they have applied a lesson because they have given the "right" answers.

The problem is, of course, that we cannot **be** Christians in Sunday school, we can only talk about it. In that sense, there is no way to apply a lesson in the classroom (except as we grow in fellowship and learn to support and encourage one another.) Sometimes there's an over-verbalization of applications in Sunday school settings which can be spiritually detrimental, or lead to false pride.

Remember that many young people and adults who come into inductive study are for the first time discovering for themselves what Jesus said and did. Frequently this information seeps into their spiritual computer like a slow charge on a battery, or like a time exposure to the Holy Spirit. So it's only gradually that they begin to see how what the Bible says makes a difference in their own lives. That's probably the most significant kind of application or life response, and you can see them being taught by the Holy Spirit even more than by you.

SHARE YOURSELF
Don Williams:

As teachers, we also need to warm up, and open up. If we're honest about our own struggles and hurts along with our triumphs, people will be helped to do this themselves.

If we are faithful in ourselves and diligent in understanding the main point of the Scripture passage, we will see the lives of our students continue to change and grow. The Holy Spirit can do marvelous things in them and us.

APPENDIX

FOR FURTHER READING

Methodical Bible Study by Robert A. Traina is the "grand-daddy" from which almost all other books on inductive Bible study come. It is a college textbook on the subject and detailed enough that you might not feel you're ready for it immediately. It is available in many Christian bookstores and from the author c/o Asbury College, Asbury, Kentucky.

A book length, college level study which demonstrates inductive Bible study on a single book is Merrill C. Tenney's *Galatians: The Charter of Christian Liberty* (Eerdmans, 1950, 1957).

There are several informal introductions to using personal inductive study and leading a group discussion. These include *Independent Bible Study* by Irving L. Jensen (Moody Press), *Personal Bible Study* by William C. Lincoln (Bethany Fellowship), *Leading Bible Discussions* by James Nyquist (Inter-Varsity Press), and *The Joy of Discovery* by Oletta Wald (Bible Banner Press). *How to Understand Your Bible* by Norton Sterret (Inter-Varsity Press) is a good introduction to reading the Bible in context and dealing with parable, figures of speech, and prophecy through an inductive approach.

Two reference tools you may want to add to your library for inductive study are a good Bible atlas and a Bible dictionary, so that you can see where something happened and find out the meaning of terms you do not know. *The MacMillan Bible Atlas* or *The Oxford Bible Atlas* are good choices, and

The New Bible Dictionary (Eerdmans) is recommended. For use with children, The Family Bible Encyclopedia (Cook, 1978) is full of pictures and simple explanations to help children explore.

Using a brief study guide on a specific book in discussion groups is probably the most popular approach to inductive study. Marilyn Kunz and Catherine Schell are co-authors of over seventeen study guides to various books of the Bible. Their series, Neighborhood Bible Studies, is published by Tyndale House and is available in almost all Christian bookstores.

Another series of guides features a variety of contributors, including Gladys Hunt, Winnie and Chuck Christensen, Margaret Fromer, and Sharrel Keyes. Called the Fisherman Bible Study Guide series, they are published by Harold Shaw Publishers, which also has an inductive series for teenagers.

Dr. Don Williams has authored a number of books to help students and beginners with inductive Bible study. These include: Celebrate Your Freedom, a study of Galatians (Word, 1975); Introduction to Inductive Bible Study, a study of Philemon (Brothers in Ministry Publishing, 1977); Journey into Joy, a study of Philippians (BIM, 1977); and The Son of Man: Studies in Mark's Gospel, a cassette tape series with study guide (Word, 1973). His other books include Call to the Streets (Augsburg, 1972), and The Apostle Paul and Women in the Church (BIM, 1977).

APPENDIX

CHOOSING A TRANSLATION

The King James Version (1611) has been for almost 400 years "the Bible." It is the most read, most quoted book in the English language, and through it millions of people have come to a saving faith. It was the first Bible that ever came into the hands of the common reader on a massive scale, after the printing press was invented. Its influence on English literature and language has been profound. But today, it has some limitations. For readers in the last part of the twentieth century, its language does not always communicate because of words and phrasings that are now obsolete and obscure. Also, because the translators did not have access to many very early Greek and Hebrew source manuscripts that we have recovered today, the scholars who formed the King James had to guess at many original word meanings which today are more clear. For these two reasons, a good modern translation brings us closer to the words and the everyday, common speech patterns of the Bible as it was originally written than the King James Version can do.

The Revised Standard Version (Old Testament, 1946, New Testament, 1952) is a revision of the 1901 American Standard Version, which attempted to solve some of the language problems of the KJV. Although some RSV wordings are in dispute, its scholarship has been sufficiently accepted so that several major denominations have adopted the RSV as their official Bible. In general, it combines clarity for the modern reader with the euphony of the King James.

The New English Bible is a modern, thoroughly scholarly translation by British scholars. The style is clear, very readable, and often catches the majesty of the KJV. This translation brings modern readers close to the wordings of the original Bible writers, within strict standards of accuracy.

The New American Standard Bible (1963) is a revision of the American Standard Version of 1901. Its scholarly accuracy cannot be disputed. It is perhaps not quite as readable as other modern translations, but for an accurate, clear modern translation, this is an excellent choice.

The Good News Bible (1976) is intended to be a Bible for all who speak English, even with a limited vocabulary. Its short, simple sentences and easy grammatical construction make it an ideal Bible for children, young people, and people for whom English is a second language, although the attempt to simplify its language so much has resulted in disagreement about the accuracy of some passages.

The New International Version (1973/78) is a major translation by an international team of English-speaking scholars that combines the accurate rendering of individual words with an attention to the total thought pattern and syntax of the original language texts. It is simple in expression, solid in scholarship, and very readable.

WHY NOT A PARAPHRASE?

Paraphrases, such as *The Living Bible* or *Phillips* version, have helped many people start reading the Bible who might not otherwise have done so. But these paraphrases were never intended to be study Bibles, and should never be used as a substitute for a translation. To paraphrase means to freely rephrase the language of the Bible text, in many cases leaving out or changing an exact, important meaning.